august witch

For the lovely Catherine
xo
[signature]

august witch

poems by Chandra Mayor

Printed and bound in Canada

Cover and book design: Rayola Graphic Design

National Library of Canada Cataloguing in Publication Data

Mayor, Chandra, 1973-
August witch : poems / Chandra Mayor.

ISBN 1-894177-12-6

I. Title.
PS8576.A958A95 2002   C811'.6   C2002-911042-4
PR9199.4.M39A95 2002

Represented in Canada by the Literary Press Group
Agented by Signature Editions

The publisher and author gratefully acknowledge the financial assistance
of the Canada Council for the Arts, the Manitoba Arts Council
and the people of Manitoba.

Cyclops Press
P.O. Box 2775
Winnipeg, MB R3C 4B4 Canada
www.cyclopspress.com

This book is for Monique and Julika

Thank you to Catherine Hunter, Clive Holden, jenn Gusberti, Kristen Adolfson, Dr. E. Tomchuk, Rachel Stone, Karen Paquin, and my family.

Special thank you to Jon Paul Fiorentino, my editor and friend.

Some of these poems have previously appeared in *dark leisure*, *Prairie Fire's Flaming Prairies: the Queer Issue*, the anthology *Exposed* (Winnipeg: The Muses Company, 2002) and *The Cyclops Review* (Winnipeg: Cyclops Press, 2002).

August Witch   9

August Witch

Cup your hands around the word: August. Press your palms together and slip between the syllables, twist and work your fingers around the letters. Release the first long moan that rises like a supplication from an open throat, like sidewalks singing shimmering in the sun. Pry into the g, exhale and tumble through the thickening air, gathering and rolling into lightning fractured skies, gulping rain with pore and tongue and leaf. Caress the little vowel, its sweet brevity belatedly remembered. And then the sibilance, the heavy-lidded indolence of s, the bacchic wasps stumbling from the nests, the split and sticky fruit and its electric trickling juices on your lips and chin and snaking down your hands. Snap your fingers sharp against the t while asters blaze and trees begin to flick the first orange leaves in crackling puddles at your feet.

Hold this in your mouth before you speak. Taste this word. It's as reverent as a carrot stretching swollen in the ground, full and firm as corn beneath the husk. It's as bitter as beer and trembles in delicious agony like sleep and apples and suspended breath.

Cup your hands around this humming buzzing word with scrabbling fingers, and abandon. Scatter the sounds like dandelion seeds, stubborn and ephemeral as blazing eyes, opened wide and rooted to this newly birthed and fierce, loamy body.

August cannot contain itself. Words and worlds split like pods of promises, over-ripe. I clawed and caught and hooked my fingers, cleaved and burst apart and found you, child of heat and storm, abundance, exultation: August witch.

section 1

Veteran Fictions

Invitation

The decoration of failure is a small
consolation: the creeping cat, her black
hole eyes rimmed with stolen moonlight
from cracks in the blinds, glowing jaundiced
rings and temporary promises, the o
of her mouth, her white teeth, licking
tinsel from the dead and brittle tree.

Who can resist the lure of open
throat, singing backward borrowed light?
The house breathes deep and discordant,
unsynchronized humming of sleep.

How much of this is singing help
less, victim, tragedy? How much of this is slitting
tongues and hairs and picking through the needles
of already dead, under cover of unseen?

I want refraction and reflection,
indulgence: the deep swallow
of ersatz silver abundance, the descent
of tangled glinting tongues, razor

rimmed. I have failed to keep
myself whole and wholly open to you.

Inside I am rib-bound and ribboned
like a maypole with strands you cannot
grasp, a dance meant for many that I cannot
weave alone.

I have failed, this night, to include you
but I can tell you oh! It's beautiful
and I can show you invitation, infestation:

my lips stretched taut,
my mouth gurgling red songs like flowers.

I Do

At least when Sylvia Plath sunk
into blackness she raged and
fought and her red-streaked
howling became poems that tore
through her throat and fingers,
menacing and pulsing
even when she
did not.
And some read her poems and think
them self-serving or courageous, mythic
or pathetic. I know them to be none
of these, nothing so mean
or large, nothing full of portent
and portentous demons, angels.
They are simply
what she
did.

What I do is this:
I forget the names of things and the reasons
for their naming. I yell at my daughter
and then cry until I'm swollen, numb, salt-

pickled. I lose hours, thoughts,
and tax receipts. I'm always inexplicably
late, and still, ten extra minutes are enough
to drown me; no lungs can suffer
that much vast and barren air and emptiness.
Nothing can be filled indefinitely
with nothing, and one day soon I'll hear
the bloated organ pop and what I'll do,
what I'll do is this:
I'll open up my perfect ohhh, my passive
throat, a bullhorn not for words or rage,
·but just this dull insistent hiss, this leaking
damp balloon, inexorable and amplified.

I am pliable, latex, limp and icing
pink. Ask me if I want the exhalation:
I do I do
I do.

Babel

My head is a hive, paper
thin, patched with spit and sweat and
scavenged scraps of sealing wax,
faded photographs of me and
me and others I've forgotten. Bees,
hornets, and wasps rustle in the catacombs,
stupefied and slatternly in their mumbled
grief, disbelieving the severance
of thread that once clutched
abdomen to thorax; the snag of shredded
wing; the dull and brittle carpet of shed
fur; the raw glimpse of skin; the sting
squandered.

It is always the end
of August here, the humid gasp:
always the stultifying cavity
that throbs between the seasons.

I press my fingers to my temples,
try to numb the whimpering and droning.
I did not cultivate these crippled insects.

I do not want these squatters. I do not cup
my hands and proffer promises of sanctuary,
haven. They built this hive, this monstrance
to themselves, without my hands. I do not
know which other life I thought I was creating,
nor how I did not notice the construction
of this legacy of obsolescence.

This is the place you find yourself,
then, the way a body wakens on a riverbank
after a beating: ribs and tissues splintered,
swollen, self-absorbed and fluent in the babble
of untenable, the brain and tongue still stuttering
in amnesia. I am the mute and renegade
neuron, the conscious chasm gaping
before remembering, naming, speaking: *wet shattered*
boots lips me blood where help
and *here*. I am the long, thick pause
where the uninvited fall
in. I do not know how
they find me.

The labyrinth in my head is dank
and over-crowded, passageways maimed
and trepidatious. My tongue is twisted, viscous,
sometimes mistaken for honey. Sometimes
a bee with limbs intact and memories distilled
to crisp delusion will make the pilgrimage
to my mouth, declare herself a prophet,
demand a revolution: order me to speak,
to propagate, to spew her visions out like pollen.

I will not be Cassandra for these tiny, tattered
impotents. I coil my tongue and snap
them up like fly-tape, grind their insubstantial
bones into the ridges of my molars. Their message
is always the same, and does not fit inside my mouth:

*It is always June, always sharp, pristine, and barely
breathed on. The sun is a voluminous glutted
buttercup, air and eyes are nectar-sodden,
invincible, and all the grass is strewn with fat
white limbs like larva.*

When did I become the drone? I don't know
how I caught and clung to this collection,
this derangement, this disease. My hidden
legion wants me to continue their contagion
but I will file my teeth to blades, seal them up like battlements.

These are not my words, I
write. These are not my words.

You Wrote Me

You wrote me into your poem, poised
and frozen on a windowsill, and I was
mute and beautiful in the moonlight.
I was a metaphor trembling with portent.
All my treacherous limbs gleamed
in the final shudder before leaping,
plunging possibility. You sat half
a country away at a desk or a bar,
inside a constricted apartment;
you wrote the angry stars, the open
window, the indifferent city sprawled
below my feet, the cool lick of limestone
beneath my toes. You wrote your hand
into the poem, the extended palm to open
and close, receiving and releasing, pushing
me loose and snatching me up in alternate
heartbeats. You imbued everything
with the reverberations of your voice:
the city, the windowsill,
the sky. Me. You read me like a postcard
and pinned me to your page. You rolled
me from your throat, damp, reborn,

and astonished. I am voiceless, bejeweled,
and immortal, captivated by the lyric
possibilities of my own hands, my own death.

This Little Girl

This little girl files her fingernails into sharpened ovals, flecked with flaking bits of blue polish. They dart like small frantic birds when she talks, and when she cries they rake her face, unbidden, with their claws.

This little girl grows her hair long and ducks her head to hide the fading red welts striping her cheeks.

This little girl grows up around the hole in her belly. She fills it with shiny bits of flattery, the glint of sunlight on hubcaps, the interminable ticking of clocks, and cigarettes that smolder forever.

This little girl undresses for as many people as possible. She has the voice of a crow and steals anything that glitters.

This little girl lifts her foot and walks like a fist smashing an egg. She shimmers like a waterfall when she dances and never turns her back against the door. Her blood is full of hungry gaping beaks that scrape inside her indigo veins. If you ask, she arranges her lips and teeth into a smile and says she's fine.

This little girl forgets a piece of herself everywhere she goes. She grows thinner every day, brittle as a lollipop. She knows she is conspicuous in camouflage and her head is filled with noise, a cacophony of wings. Midnight constricts the air like a hand around her throat and the floor is littered with sequins. The clock turns its face away and this little girl shudders and shakes all night long.

Continue

Morning rolls onto your chest and you wake gasping
for breath and reason. Your mouth is dry and sour
and you gulp down guilt, ignore the heaps of clothes
and newspapers and shoes and books in every
corner. You have to get up. The floor is gritty as sand
beneath your bare feet and your head is heavy
on your shoulders. You are walking through water.
If you open your mouth you'll drown. The cat weaves
through your legs creating whirlpools around your ankles.
There was somewhere you meant to go, you began
with determination and a destination but you find
yourself hooked through your lip and you can't
remember the reason for the struggle. The sun
is excruciatingly slow as it spins across the sky.
Your house is filled with wreckage and debris
and your thoughts are barely glimpsed
through silty water. Your heart hammers
fists under your ribs but the way to continue
living is to stand very still. The way to continue
breathing is not to scream. The way to continue
fighting is to acquiesce to meaninglessness,
aimlessness, and terror. You find yourself a way.

Crisis House

1.
The First Time

The first time was because of my tongue, the way it settled in my mouth like a slug, silent and glistening. The sun shone in squares through the dirty window and I sat in stasis on the green couch for hours, forfeit to gravity, all my molecules engorged and motionless.

This is what it's like to be a drum full of oil.

I could hear my lover on the phone with my doctor, with my mother, making arrangements.

This is what it's like to be a vase of flowers filled with stagnant water.

They decided that there was no point in going to the hospital; they wouldn't admit me, I wasn't a danger to myself or others, I was merely entropied and mute.

This is what it's like to be a tree contemplating the chainsaw.

My lover packed an overnight bag for me, all the ordinary fixtures of my life suddenly ridiculous: the pink shirt stolen from the dark cave of drawers, balls of socks for severed feet. The world disappeared every time I blinked and I was grateful.

This is what it's like to watch fireworks on the insides of your eyelids.

We got in the car and drove to a little white house in St. Boniface. The back door was locked and we had to ring the bell to be admitted. I was taken to a bedroom, hospital issue bed, desk, chair. A young woman went through my bag, touched all my clothes, looking for sharps. She took away my medication and my lighter and my glass bottle of sandalwood. I sat on the bed with my knees drawn up and my face in my hands, afraid to speak, forgetting how to nod.

This is what it's like to be a nightcrawler, limbless and pink, dug out of the earth.

My lover held my hand and then she left. The door was closed. My breath was tangled in my ribs and I could only quietly gasp. I slept in all my clothes, sitting up against the wall. I mutely accepted my pills at ten o'clock. There was a black hole in the sky where the moon should have been. No one else came to the door and I was glad and terrified.

This is what it's like to wake up in a snowbank with a mouth full of blood, your tongue in someone else's hand. This is what it's like to be bone in the moment before it shatters. This is what it's like to be a rock waiting for the body.

2.
House

This is an ordinary house, plastered
with a calm mask of white stucco.
This house is flanked with other white
houses trimmed in blue, green, or red.
This house hides a wooden swing
in the back, a picnic table, a parking
pad, and is hemmed in with an impenetrable
brown fence. On the other side of the fence
is a daycare, and sitting at the back
of this house, smoking a cigarette
and sweating under the merciless sun,
you can hear the children screeching
and you hate them.

This is a mundane house with a large
bay window clouded with curtains like
cataracts. This is a house that never looks
at the park across the street, the sagging
trees, the red and yellow snapdragons.
This is a tidy house with a prim green
lawn, eschewing window boxes,

unadorned. This is a house you drive
past every day and do not see.
This is a house where you are incapable
of looking up.

This is a house that squats stupidly and says
nothing. This is a house with eavestroughs
full of spiders. This is a house that models
banality and flaunts its ordered shingles
to the neighbours.

You are in crisis.

3.

The Second Time

The second time was because we'd fought about something that I forget
and I cried and cried and I couldn't stop crying even in my psychia-
trist's office I cried and couldn't speak and he told me that if I didn't
speak he'd have to put me in the hospital and I didn't want to go there
so I said *No* and he called the crisis house instead and administered the
intake questionnaire over the phone while I dumbly nodded or shook
my head

Have you ever tried to hurt yourself
Have you ever committed arson
Have you ever used street drugs
Have you ever committed homicide
Are you suicidal Are you suicidal Are you suicidal

My lover came to pick me up and I was still crying but I put my hands
over my face to hide the bloody scratches on my cheeks and of course
you can't ever really die from shame and she was worried and I was
ashamed and she took time off work and I was ashamed and she drove
me to the crisis house and I lay on the bed with my silent earphones on
to make them think I couldn't hear them and I cried and my roommate
tried to get a nurse because I wouldn't stop crying but I heard the nurse
outside the door she said *Crying is what we do here, dear* and I knew I

was flattened against a wall and I knew no one would touch me gently and I'd hit them if they tried and I knew I had to keep up my guard and I thought *fuck all of you* and I wailed like a child and I cried and I cried and I cried

as generous and impersonal as rain

4.
Veteran Fictions

They leave me with the mirror and the light
bulb in the desk lamp. The click of the closing door
is precise, remonstrative: a snapping finger, a locking
chamber, precursor to panic. I strip the bed and smother
the light bulb in a blanket before I step on it; I know
that everyone hears everything and they're all listening
through the walls, eavesdropping on the snuffling
of someone else's despair, despite themselves.
I'm determined that I will not be discovered. I unbundled
the blanket and the shattered glass rasps against itself
in a small opaque mosaic. There's a picture, there's a message,
there's a narrative that emerges from this fragmentation and it
whispers *touch me touch me touch me* and trembling
I answer *yes.* My arms are so cooperative, the veins throwing
themselves against the skin, urging liberation, urging passion,
the long sharp pain, hair line thin, the indrawn breath.

This is the crimson deluge of insensibility, the reclamation of
my body, purging entropy and piecing myself together inside-out.
This is what it's like inside a waterfall, the torrent in your ears,
the rolling of your body over rocks and rapids. This is what it's like

to bleed to death, alone. This is what it's like to be released,
to cry and cry in rage and shame, impotent, forgotten.

I lie underneath the blanket, skin itching
against the wool, cowardice licking the tears
from my eyes and the desk lamp bleeding
light, all the shadows unvanquished. This is
only what I wish I'd done, my secret,
sweet and warm, my scarred and veteran fictions.

5.
Benediction

This is a benediction for your ambulatory
body, a blessing on both the legs that carried
you through the door and up the stairs.
You went forth and shattered and your shards
of self increased a thousand-fold but o
your skin sealed you up and only split
a little at the seams, and you came
back. This house welcomes you like a mouth
and caresses you like swallowing, your swollen
eyes and overnight bag, your toothbrush
and your confiscated matches, consecrated.
Don't hold out your clammy palms in supplication.
Receive gladly that which you are given.
There will be no concessions. This is the hallowing
of fear and shame, the suspension of time, the cataloging
of your failures made flesh, and crying, upstairs
and alone on a cast-off hospital bed, your own futile
invocations of grace spiraling, heavy and hollow,
inside your ears. This is a blanket to cover
yourself, this is a blessing, benediction.

section 2

Marked

Marked

If you know enough to linger,
I'll offer up the stories of my winter mouth.
My lips are dry chapped braille,
smooth as polished fingernails
with sharpened tips and ragged cuticles.
I'll crack and catch you unaware,
punctuate the licking tongue that reads
the words I've spit into the wind.
The corners of my mouth that split
into my cheeks are filled with ice
and will not heal, reopening
with every word I speak, every story
that I tell or choose to choke on.

By April I'll have different text to offer,
but don't mistake me for exceptional:
there are no unmarked bodies.

Ascension

When I was skin stretched taut
around my bones, I swung my thighs
like scythes as I walked through crowded
streets, heels striking the pavement and sparking
like flint, the soles of my shoes never flat
against the sidewalk. My spine lurched
from my back in bas relief and I tried to climb
it like a ladder, crawl out through my throat
and drift away, dissipate like smoke. My eyes
were round and glassy as marbles and they gobbled
up my face; I pursed my lips and swallowed only
pills and coffee. My lover clutched the little
bones of my finger like the string of a balloon;
I hoarded all the household pins and played secret
naughts and crosses on my ankles and my wrists.
I closed my eyes like wings against my cheeks
and whispered *feathers luminescence helium
ascension.* Longing for erasure, I scoured my heavy
hands in bleach but learned that fingerprints are stubborn,
sticky little maps into yourself. I could not rub away
the ridges, slough out of the labyrinth. I curled
up naked on the gleaming bathroom floor and cried

razor-edged tears for my shivering, clattering bones; my self-inflicted shreds of flesh; the heaviness of salt. I was light years from the nearest constellation.

Correspondence

I can't claim ownership of my body.
At best we have an uneasy truce,
renegotiated with every uneven
patch of pavement, every crowded
street, every heated throbbing
bass line, seducing my hips and urging
me to dance floors teeming with feet.

This body and I frequently betray each
other. Each of us have honed our skills
and strategies of petty revenge into instinctive
art forms. We've learned that skin
is a canvas receptive to knives and needles,
fingernails and flame. We send each other cryptic
postcards, etched in scars and stretching wrinkles.
My favourites are the unexpected gifts, slyly,
clandestinely planned and delivered instantly:
riots of tender flowers, blossoming purple,
yellow, green across my flesh.

These velvety, bruised bouquets are never
accompanied with a card, but o
my secret, deviant admirer:
I'd know your fingerprints
anywhere.

What to Do About the Scars

You need the long sleeve shirts that button firmly
at the wrist, the ones that can be trusted
to follow your hand, acquiescent, even when you stretch
or point. You need a large watch with a thick
metal band, cool against your skin, or else
the subtle embrace of leather, fat and supple.
That still leaves the other arm to contend
with, and then there's summer, when sweat clings
thick to leaves and upper lips, trees and tube
tops wilt, and secret dripping and slight moaning
stirs the only breath of air. Your long sleeves will not last
July unnoticed, unremarked by your neighbours
and your boss, the knowing stares of strangers
at the bus-stop. The problem's solved with bracelets:
you can say they're sentimental, braids of leather,
knotted thread, green that bleeds into the yellow,
blue, four inches thick. You wear them all
the time, say the shower's made them stiff. You say
I have a lot of friends, each one a covenant.
It's good to have some metal bangles, too, thin
and silver, marked with delicate lines of leaves,
twisted flowers; the precision of the engraving will lure

your finger. The continuity of unbroken lines,
the complicated intricacy is pleasing. It's better
still if one of them has a ragged edge inside
the band, a mistake, a sharp piece of metal
the artisan forgot to file. Or maybe it wasn't carelessness,
she knew and left it for you, hidden gift, double
edged. While your finger strokes the vines, you're etching
blood threaded bracelets, not quite deep enough to drip. Circles
lapping circles are what weave you to yourself. You spin
the bracelets slowly, you can do this anywhere and this pleases
you. People think you smile a lot, say that you're so friendly,
so unique, such a character. The jangle of tiny bells follows
you everywhere.

Tattoos and Triggers

1.

Not all tattoos are permanent. The harbourage
of ink may be provisional, dependant on resiliency
of mooring, susceptibility of locations where the body
will perpetually relinquish and regenerate the flesh:
nescient, neoteric, certain pieces of yourself
that you can hardly call your own except in past
or future tense. A tattoo on the inside of your lip
will eventually be chewed or licked away,
although the timing's imprecise and unreliable;
aridity or generosity of the human mouth
are climacteric variables, volatile and unpredictable.

The most practical and transitory place
to practice inking is the bottom of your feet:
rosy pads of toes, firm and rounded,
callused soles, treacherous lazarets. This requires
flexibility of tendons, some contortion, but
any awkward, undesired line or imperfection
will shed and fade with each successive sloughing,
yielding layer. And if that's still too gradual

and gentle, you crave quicker, self-controlled
corrosion of the stain, let your bare feet seek
out sidewalks, gravel, concrete:
walk away.

2.

Duct tape, ink and extra needles, extricate
the slender cartridge from a pen, leave
the hollow plastic throat, clear and scratched
and gaping. A motor, modified, one that nestles
in your palm: an old electric razor, headless,
without blades. A rubber band for tension,
regulation of inevitable advancement and return.
A thigh, a breast, an ankle, any naked fleshy
morsel. An electrical socket within arm's reach.
There's nothing secret, complicated, in the
requirements of equipment, nothing you don't own,
unknowingly, nothing that your hands have never
touched. The bits and pieces of the tattoo gun
lie dormant in your bathroom, purse, and kitchen.

Implementation requires another kind of scavenging,
of gathering. Sometimes they'll bring a picture,
asking faithful replication. Sometimes they'll select
your standard flash, simple transfer, tracing. Rarely,
you're allowed to choose the mark, presented
with a blank and passive canvas, precious gift.
More often, you interpret, seek form and pattern

in instruction, plot with patience, colours, lines.
You listen and determine how to manifest precisely
what's already been imagined, technicolour odds
and ends in someone else's mind. It's design and divination,
and then the skin itself is hard to see, cluttered
with description and desire. You pry the pulsing
needle of the gun below the surface, create,
connect the lines, visible and blatant. You conjure
boundaries and images, confer indelibility
despite the body's slow erosion, the flaking off
of excess tissue, the atrophy of cells, disappearance.

Some people turn the gun onto themselves,
but few can bear that kind of culpability.
They'll come to you, instead, for intimate
invasion, demarcation, saying *Make me
unmistakable, intransigent, uncommon.*
You fill the gun with ink, plug the cord
into the socket. You flick the power on,
let the harsh electric groaning
permeate the room.

3.

I had a homemade gun, or rather, I had
several. They varied by the usefulness or sophistication
required or desired. Not the kind with sight and bullets,
though. If you wanted homemade weapons
there are quicker, easier things you can create.
Besides, there's no intimacy in the firing
of a gun, nothing human. They're for cowards
and assassins, amateurs. You never even need
to get involved.

The most effective weapon is the victim's own body.
For example, pay diligent attention, exploring softly,
gentle practice – your thumb will learn precisely
where to burrow between the eyeball and its socket,
knuckle deep. Then it's just a flick, a grunt, a flip.
There are other sweet and tender places, too,
full of ache: the base of the throat, under the chin,
things you never thing about, or think I never
think about.

I'm not afraid to get too close. The muscles
in my fingers have grown long and hard and
greedy. I know that bodies will betray themselves
with precious little coaxing, just a bit of well-placed
pleasure, deliberate pressure. It's never knives and guns
that kill, nor the crowbar or the slashing broken
bottle. At heart it's all that generosity of burbling
and gurgling, spitting out the blood, never knowing
when to quit – always the body's dumb extravagance
that throws it all away, does it in.

Still, we let ourselves be touched with tenderness,
without flinching. We leave our brash and hopeful
skins exposed, arrogant and enticing, vulnerability
pooled like sweat in crease of knee and elbow,
shimmering in the shadows of our foolish
naked eyes. This blitheness, these coy grins,
this utter lack of decency or caution is an inexcusable
display. Even that word, *victim*, is a lie:
we do it to ourselves. We are designed to break and
stutter, stagger, pulse, and leak away. Never trust
or underestimate a body, especially
your own.

Broken

"She taught me that women who want without needing are expensive and sometimes wasteful, but women who need without wanting are danger-ous—they suck you in and pretend not to notice." —Audre Lorde

I need without wanting, and do not want this need. Fondling
the guillotine of abstraction, I cleave with the delusion
of ordered neatness and controlled order: self-circumcision.

I do not acknowledge the pounding hunger that ruptures
moist moth-wing skin; the aching winding torture
of systems subverted, veins and arteries wrenched
and realigned to the medusa knot between my legs;
the involuntary parting of my thighs; my duplicitous
mouths gaping, baring crimson-drenched and feral teeth.

I am grasping for the firm and slippery sirens; they lure
me into thunderous salted oceans of hands and wrecks
and brine. The slightest provocation will release
my headless body to breast wave after wave after wave:
wash up broken and whole on some pink and tender shore.

Nightdiving: Tongue in Cheek

Facedown in the shallows lapping sleep,
one final breath to plunge my lungs in brine
before I leap with aching arch of spine
and clench my teeth against my oyster mouth.

This is a photograph I keep in black and black
of ocean-thrashed debris behind the sun, and deep within
you'll see my voice dislodge thick-muscled tongue
with siren songs I've left unsung to roll from cheek to cheek
and gather speed and membranes.

I know the shape and taste of urgency grown
in sunlight and saliva to shatter teeth.
Each click of consonant, caress of o
is spun in groans and mucus in my throat.
I pulse in salted heat.
The ocean moans the motion of my labour;
compulsion-gripped we part my lips:
undone and spewing scream-scorched pearls at sun,
my voice is hungry bone-loved blood.
I heave and call and come and come and come.

The Moon is Always

The moon is always you, and I am drawn
to trace the ripe crescent swelling around
your hip, the arc of your throat, the classic curve
of your eyes, and the velvet indigo shadows beneath.

You are always the moon, and I ache in your
absence, although you never leave me for long,
lingering late into the morning and ascending
again in the afternoon, balm for my sun-blind eyes.

The moon is waxen, bloodless.
The moon does not have your mouth.
The moon does not contain your breath.

You are never the moon, but your dimpled
skin is luminescent, it gleams and lures my gaze,
my hands, and I am always reaching for you.

The moon is never you, but I arch to your rhythms
all the same, and I weep relief with the crashing
tidal pool upon your every return.

The moon has a profile that changes with perspective,
and I have written encrypted love poems within
its every dimple and shadow, secrets that borrow
light from our love making to illuminate
the stars and blaze our skins and stories across the sky.

This moon is only for us.

section 3

Absent

Cary and the Mountains

1.

Before Cary moved to Banff she tore a picture of the mountains from an old *National Geographic.* The inside paper edges relinquished the binding like ragged moth wings, and rasped an imperfect fit, leaving small white gaps and displaced trees that towered without trunks, or sprouted improbable branches and arms from nowhere. We took the inner seam on faith and taped the edges together anyway. My small daughter ate a cheese sandwich and I bent over the trail of crumbs scattered over the dirty linoleum, while Cary taped the picture to the fridge. *See baby?* she said, *That's where I'm going. Cary's going to the mountains.* My daughter tasted the new word and handed me her crusts. I put them in the pile of crumbs and bent my body into the broom. Cary bent her body into my back, I leaned into the warm length of her, and we practiced imperfectly the rhythms of sweeping.

2.

After Cary moved to Banff my daughter would ask me, daily, where she was. We'd stand together in front of the picture on the fridge and I'd say, *See the mountains, baby? Cary's in the mountains.* She'd look for Cary in the glossy evergreens while I explained that mountains are as big as the sky, and very far away. Walking together through this flat and steady city, three weeks later, she asked me if the TD tower was a mountain and I told her, *Mountains have no windows.* I taught her to look down, feel the stolid assurance of prairie streets through the soles of her feet. After a month without Cary, I drove my daughter to the perimeter, taught her to look forward forever at the horizon. The sunset was interminable, aching, indolent. She fell asleep in the car. Later that night, in bed, she insisted we wrap each other tight near the edge, an empty white expanse of sheet beside us. *Leave a space for Cary.*

3.

Cary spent three months in Banff, then followed summer further west, unpacked her duffle bag in Vancouver. Four months after that I told my small daughter, now a little bigger, that we were going to visit Cary in the mountains. My daughter couldn't comprehend the flight and speed of airplanes. I pointed out the window and said, *See baby? Look down and see how tiny everything is, how high we are, how fast we go.* But it was already November, the snow had fallen, and for the length of two provinces it was hard to tell the clouds from the ground. I knew the brown blotches marring the miles of snow were the roofs of peoples' homes, or just trees who'd lifted their limbs to us, frozen and imploring. I said, *Baby, look at the snow. It's like we're flying through a book without pictures, and you can tell me how the story goes.* That didn't interest her very much so she pestered the stewardess for more crayons, especially *yellow*, *green*, and *red*. I thought of all the aborted poems I'd tried to write, their sharp unfinished corners splintered in my throat. I fed my daughter gummi-worms when the pressure in her ears became piercing and unbearable, made her cry.

4.

After my daughter and I had flown forever above the winter prairie sprawling white and flat and indistinguishable, interminable, Alberta blossomed unannounced beneath us in gray irregular patches, seamed with black. From this height it might have been just dirty snow sullied with permeable margins, interpretation, speculation, but I got excited anyway. I said, *Look, baby, mountains.* She was excited too until she'd stared at all that gray and didn't see Cary. Then she remembered that I'd told her *Mountains are as big as the sky*, and we were in an airplane in the sky, and the mountains were below us, and she knew I'd lied to her twice. I thought about the way that words can bleed into each other, the distortions of perspective, expectations, optical delusions. I saw how tall my daughter was and thought I'd drown in all the questions in her eyes. I sighed and handed her the gummi-worms, told her it could be her own special job to find Cary in the airport.

5.

After the plane landed in Vancouver with my growing daughter and me inside it, the airport swallowed us up and tightened its throat. I scanned all the eyes for Cary's, but my daughter saw her first and squealed. Even when Cary smiled at me, I almost didn't recognize her beneath the unfamiliar shirt, the different-coloured hair. There wasn't enough money for a taxi so we hauled our bags out to the bus-stop, rode in jolts and stops and starts into the city. My daughter was exhausted and enthralled, full of crackling curiosity, and asked a million questions faster than we could answer. Cary didn't know she'd learned to speak in sentences. My tongue felt like a rock and I felt flat beneath it. There was a small space between our bodies on the bus seat; only the bones of our elbows and knees could find each other. When the bus stopped suddenly my daughter fell and wedged her squirming sturdy body beneath the seat in front of her. She began to howl *Mommy Mommy Mommy I'm stuck*, her bewilderment and outrage etched sharply with fatigue. Cary and I laughed, electric, and everything was blurred confusion, motion. My head banged into someone's arm and I stomped on Cary's toe, heard her gasp, trying to pull my daughter out.

6.

Visiting Cary in Vancouver, we camouflaged the spaces in our conversation with cigarettes and fumbling for matches. Evening found us perched on plastic chairs on the flat and pebbled roof of the garage, encouraging raspy purring half-grown cats to linger on our separate laps while my daughter slept in the basement. I noticed that Cary looked up a lot. For her, the sky could be languorous and ephemeral, could drift and drape itself along the mountain peaks, never worry about falling. Looking up made me squint, made my eyes feel hot and itchy. Even when I shut them I could feel the panic circling, I could feel the jagged peaks looming and encroaching. I knew they were implacable, unyielding. I couldn't see beyond what was in front of me, and I hated the way they gobbled up the sun before I'd gotten warm or said goodnight.

7.

After we'd visited Cary in Vancouver and flown back across the prairie into winter, my daughter told everyone she met about the mountains and Cary's cats, the purring that erupted from the darkness of their bellies. When we moved to a new apartment we left the picture of the mountains still taped together on the fridge. My daughter didn't ask about it; I assume that someone peeled and picked the tape, threw it all away, wiped the surface clean. I fingered all my torn and tender edges like a rosary or a broken tooth, until they weren't so sharp, stroked and worried round and smooth, familiar. So did Cary. Now when we talk on the phone, late at night when we can afford the cost of a long-distance call, our voices bounce against each other like a string of beads with tiny echoes. We've conceded to the pauses, delicate, considerate, and cautious, learned to bend around them.

Tender

The stiffening leaves shred the morning light like razors, and fragments of the sun lie strewn between the trees, beneath my feet. Everything green is souring at the edges, and one large bush relinquishes yellow leaves the size of my palms, like lily pads or pancakes on the pavement. Do you remember September in this city? The world turns upside down, the tree limbs claw the sky and the leaves all leap to rustle and cluster at the trunk. All these tiny, crisp deaths. My breath hovers around my mouth like a ghost; if I exhale from the bottom of my lungs it just floats away and dissipates. I can't hold on to anything at this time of year; words and keys and lovers slip away, or crumble, desiccated, brittle in my hands. You wouldn't even recognize me: my fingernails are orange, misshapen and irregular as pumpkins, and I bleached my hair a yellow shade of apricot. I've learned my lessons from squirrels and from grieving, and dispersed most of my memories of you in hidden pockets and obscure cavities in my mind; even in desolation there are crevices I've forgotten and will never stumble on. Look, I need to confess: this morning I stepped on one of the last sluggish summer wasps, and I remembered you. You used to say it was a kind of euthanasia for these hungry, half-dead insects, your heavy foot a mercy. Perhaps it only had a day or two of life left to it anyway, a few ragged gasps before the next snap of cold. But staring at these crushed remains, this furred and flattened bit of sunshine on the sidewalk, I need to tell you this:

It's a killing nonetheless, and even in this season of brilliance and surrender, there is no tenderness in hastening decay.

Anemia

1.

Plasmic prankster deprivations fool
you into subsisting on exhaustion, drooping
eyes and groggy limbs, while the blood
hungers for thunder and substance.

To take iron into my system I could eat
cityscapes of towered horizons, pick
my teeth with the girdings left to prop
up the unfinished skeletons that wait
for morning, weary and wary,
pale and bleached in the moonlight.

I could snake on my belly, lick
a prairie's length of railroad tracks.
I could plant myself on all fours
in the mountains, spread wide
my sly and gaping mouth:
wild trickster with hair bristling
like spruce and thistle. The train will never believe
I am not a tunnel and will slam screeching and
sparking down my throat.

O lovely lovely
I lick my lips with glee,
relish the black grease on my tongue.

2.

Megan makes plans for a doctor's appointment
to check her ration of iron. Needing to quantify
the level of her hunger, she's willing to welcome
the silver stab, the draining, the needle's
measured appropriation in her vein.

It's a pity she can't directly trade the carefully
labeled vial for the styrofoam-clasped liver
at the supermarket: a bit of blood for bits of flesh.

At midnight Megan's still in the kitchen. The air
is thick and dark with onions and liver, fried in oil
and moonlight. Pale fingers pick morsels from the pan.

Upstairs her grandmother's throat tightens in sleep.
She dreams of her mother, and her own stomach's
violent rebellion, betrayal, and refusal of sustenance
and sacrifice. She knows she is turned inside-out
and empty, and she is never sufficiently grateful
for that which she has been given.

Megan feels the masses multiply inside her;
their clamouring crowds her throat. She knows
she is experiencing a minor miracle:
she will feed them all with flesh barely
warm and she can't stop eating.

Sweet Mouthful

We light all the candles, even in the afternoon when winter
sun burns through the window of your apartment,
brittle and opaque as icicles. These rooms are full
of photographs and smell of clean. We drink
out of wine glasses, cupped full and rounded
as the moon on a stem, our fingers as long and elegant
as any shooting star. After each sweet mouthful
the world clicks into focus like the consonants
in our conversation or the fracture of beads and light
inside a kaleidescope, the way the snapping of a twig
in the cold lifts your eyes to the entire ice-encased
and clutching tree. We are not two women drinking
in the afternoon. We are not afraid to go outside
and leave the candles burning. We are full of wit
and insight, we are laughing and compassionate.
Our slender cigarettes, left burning in the ashtray,
breathe intransparent rings into the air, and our eyes
are round and clear and extraordinarily bright.
We are captivated by our beauty and invulnerable
to the frailties of our friends, burning hot and hard
as fallen stars in the snow. The precision of our

sentences sting like sleet, and the clarity of our vision
strips the world, encircled in our arms.

Even after I have left and you are sleeping, glasses
rinsed and upside-down beside the sink, these things
linger, frozen like a snapshot: the imprint of our bodies
on the furniture, the open-throated possibilities
we imagined, the yellow stain of nicotine on paint,
the sweet allure of warmth and fleeting comprehension.

Luminous

I will write on the face of the moon and send
you luminous etchings of this silent city quieted
in pale and stinging snowfall; rounded moss-
velvet cheek of child, rosy and rolled in sleep
and dreams and blankets; my own face
learning the contours of hope.

I will find the words to write to you in petal-flurries
of the wings of birds that rise from my belly and
my blood, birthing stars from my throat. As the fingers
of your voice draw me into you, I will feed on your
laughter, fall into your silences, and harbour
you in luminosity. Until you speak again,
I will catch you vibrant and dancing in the shimmering
purple-green of northern lights, my waiting arms
encircling you as horizon makes covenant with sky.

Wreckage

Today I am walking myself
to school, my daughter announces.

       Six is too little to cross
       the busy street, I tell her. *No,*
       I tell her. *No, we're late.*
Yes, she says:
my own flat voice perfectly
mimicked and detonated
by her small mouth, filled
with silver.

She is the alchemist of her bendable
bones, her ribs a granite cave
to bulwark lungs and larynx,
stone firmament of breath that forges
words implacable, the tone
that threatens with imper:meability.

My tone. My voice. My last defense
against assault. Her body knows this,
knows offense, knows my own blue
eyes will grid themselves with iron splinters,
gray. Her toes have told her of the strata
beneath snow and dirt and concrete,
taught her irises the countenance
of continents of stone that do not blink.

I know that look, that gaze, the precise
instinctive measurement of narrowed eyelids.
I've never seen my eyes displaced
before, surrounded by another face, controlled
and occupied by some one else.

>   *Come on, we're late, I've had enough,*
>   I say. *We have to go.*
No, she says,
>   and *Yes,* I say,
like she said,
I said,
minutes before.

This movement is a continental shift. The earth collides
with itself, shudders, quakes; land and people fall
off the edges of the world, swallowed by oceans,
buried in rubble. Victims who survive the devastation
are incomprehensible, maimed, burdened with ghosts
of limbs and siblings, cities, houses, heirs, wretched wreckage.

My stomach clenches and shudders, the snowflakes
tremble on our eyelashes. There are struggling fears
and secrets in my daughter's veins, devastations
I know she'll never tell me.

Scavenger

I'm always hungry, ravenous, by the time we get
home in the evening. Now the days are getting longer
again, stretched and taut, tenacious. The sun hooks
fingernails into the thin pale sky and clutches
at an extra twenty minutes, half an hour. The sky is free
of snow and other meat and matter, and offers sparse
resistance or enticement. My stomach is a hollow globe
streaked with copper-tainted acid, restrained by membranes
soaked in mucus, it gurgles threats and lullabies
beneath my voice. I am a duet that speaks
of muddy boots and sparkling floors, singing
the counterpart of emptiness: ravage, ravish, rage,
devour.

I sit wedged into the spine of the sofa,
fat recipe book propped open on my knees,
flip the glossy pages with moistened finger.
Saddle of Lamb with Artichoke Puree, Cooked Hearts
Of Palm, Beef-On-Tomato Medallions: the illustrations
have fought with dust and faded to orange and pink,
coral, the hams match my lipstick, waxy,
smug. The hardwood floors gleam, steeped

in the remnants of light, and my daughter spins
in grubby socks in circles, chanting *chocolate
cake chocolate cake chocolate cake*. My girlfriend treads
an asymmetrical orbit around us, gathering laundry
from floor and furniture. Her hamper overflows
and there's still a sock smirking and crumpled behind the t.v.

There's nothing in the recipe book to feed
me, nothing but fractions and precision, implicit
threats crooned beneath a thousand impenetrable
synonyms for cut and cook, step-by-step instructions.
The consequence of extravagance, circumvention,
substitution trembles in the antonym of adjectives: stringy,
tough and blackened, fallen. The fruit of infidelity
is failure, inedible disaster. Juices tumbling
over the tongue and sustenance burgeoning in the heavy
gut are offered only to the meticulous,
the scrupulous, the constant and the faithful cook.
I am none of these.

Instead I scavenge odds and ends from freezer,
cupboard, fridge. I fill the roasting pan
with plump orange disks of carrots, naked wet
potato orbs, pepper and green celery confetti, pearly
onion hula hoops, strips of pork fried in oil and garlic
from pink and limp to firm luminosity. My daughter
circles me like a squawking buzzard, my girlfriend
emerges bearing lemony laundry from the basement
precisely at the moment that the sky's last bloody
rend is licked away with violet darkness. The beer
is bitter, golden, swallow deeply once
before emptying the stout green bottle into the fecund
jumble in the pan, dream of getting drunk of vegetables,
bits of meat, saliva streaming like lust and fever as we gather
in the kitchen, nostrils flaring.

An hour later, by the light of the television, I serve
it up with toasted buns dripping butter, thick sweet
dollops, paint all our bellies the colour of bloated
dandelions, hiccuping excess and stuffed and sated
until morning. I gather them into my arms and food and
feast and feed them, corpulent in my greed and crammed
and glowing with my riches.

Rivers

1.

Like all good prairie girls, I wanted to grow up to
be a spinning figure skater. My father worked one
winter for a week to shovel snow off of the river,
down to ice. He built a rink for me on the frozen
Red. I thought this gift was beautiful, lucky lucky
little girl with her private winter river. But my
leather-wrapped and silver-bladed feet rebelled.
The river ice was black and bumpy, marred with
frozen fissures, cracks. Underneath lurked something
wild and transient, hungry currents wide-awake
and clutching at me. Dad promised it was safe but I was
frozen and ashamed. I longed for indoor ice, soft
and white and sprayed with neat red lines, the community
rink we'd left behind in the country. I knew the river
never really slept. I knew its bottomless treachery,
the forever-away it would take me, given the chance.

2.

My dad grew up on Tremblay Street in St. Boniface, suspended
between the meat packing plant and the river. It was the small
river, the wrong river: the Seine, that fickle abundance that ebbs
into the weedy trickle, the joke. He trapped a beaver on its banks
once, brought it home in a box; another gift gone awry, it attacked
his best friend's dog so he took it back. He tied a piece of bacon
to a string, dipped it in the river and pulled up crayfish; wary
of their pincers, he threw them back, sometimes gave them
to a neighbour to use as bait for larger, unsuspecting fish.
The Tremblay kids had a pick-up football team, the no-tackling
rule forgotten halfway into the game. My dad once
played with a three-day-old broken collarbone; *We were*
tougher then, he tells me. He is full of pranks and stories
bound against the river, and Tremblay is a street of ghosts:
my Nana dropping out of a tree onto the neighbourhood bully,
my uncle and the future high school principal stealing
my dad's car, plotting escape, gunning over the river
on the green footbridge, getting stuck halfway across,
forced to confess.

3.

I spent my childhood transplanted from a small town
to St. Boniface. My parents bought a house in Norwood
Flats, on Lyndale Drive. The gaping picture window,
the clipped and shadowy lawn, the Drive, the trailed
and leafy riverbank, the self-assured and careless Red,
flung forward in a linear optical path from inside the quiet
living room that we only sat in during holidays. I hated
the city: the fluoride water, the kids in cliques I couldn't
penetrate, and all the trees that grew for shade and for
aesthetics, not for climbing. I cried myself to sleep for
the house we'd left behind, the wildflowers and ditches,
the acres in the country. The Flats were crammed with
curtain-shrouded eyes that watched me while I played, and so I
stopped. When my little brother went to kindergarten,
he peed against the trees on Lawndale's boulevard.
A neighbour called our house, and my mom explained
about the city's rules, but he couldn't understand.

4.

The Seine cut through the wrong side of St. Boniface:
no gyms or stadiums, high schools or money. My dad,
athletic star, had never seen a basketball until he walked
just over a mile to the school beside the Red: the other
river, full and throaty, cross-hatched with hidden
currents. The brown inscrutable waters promised
affluence and advantage, the annual smug swelling
of bloated confidence. While the Great Flood threatened
devastation, homes on the Red were fortified and sand-bagged;
the city watched the Flats with indrawn breath and worry.
Newspapers sent photographers, immortalized the scene
in black and white. City-planners prioritized the dangers,
designated Tremblay as the edge of the known world, not
worth the effort, sacrificed. Grandpa worked up north
then, in a factory. Nana would not cede her wringer-washer,
just acquired and long saved-for. She ascended with it
from the basement dug-out; her five-foot frame still
can't explain the sudden strength, saviour of the washer
and three children, mistress of the clean-up and rebuilding.
My dad was six. At sixteen, at the high school near
the Red, he had not forgotten.

5.

Genetically betrayed, I was hopeless in gym, picked
last for every team. Basketballs leapt away from
me like slippery planets on erratic, unfathomable
orbits. There were so many rules I didn't understand,
and my street was too consumed by green abundant
lawns to have a sidewalk for practicing. I got lost
in poetry instead, tried to write on the summer
riverbank but mosquitoes drove me back into my
bedroom. I filled pages and pages of my journal
with poems of Paris, London, Bangkok, places
I'd never seen.

6.

My father's high school stories are full of will
and hours of walking to and from the school
and practices and the Red Top. He was called
The Fox, captained all the teams; all the mothers
of my childhood friends had harboured secret
crushes. He proved himself every day to the kids
from the Flats, back and forth across the Seine,
steely-eyed and fierce against the Red. His stories
filled my mouth with bitterness, injustice. I wrote
the secret subtext of envy, hatred for the Red,
the thoughtless gifting of geography, children of privilege.

7.

When I was thirteen someone set fire to my dad's
old high school so my parents sent me somewhere
else, a school beside the Assiniboine. My new
classmates spent vacations in Aruba, Aspen,
South America, and couldn't comprehend
station wagons, camping. At night I walked
downtown across two bridges and two rivers
to a café referred to by mother only as that *den
of iniquity*: the Blue Note, smoky, dark, and strange.
The walk was long and cold, my path compelled
by the injustice of her words, the secret sweetness
of boundaries transgressed, the hard lick of
danger, determination.

8.

At fifteen I brought my bed and clothes and books
across the rivers to a Broadway apartment. I left
my parents together, empty-handed, in the house
with the riverview blurred and softened by the sheer
ivory drapes. I learned the downtown orbits, crossed
over the Red again only occasionally for laundry
or to pilfer food. They divorced and sold the house;
I haven't seen the Flats for years. Grandpa died
and Nana sold the Tremblay house, moved into
a highrise. I remember all the stories that the rivers
structured and punctuated, the misalignments
of desire and escape. We all escaped somehow,
dispersed and moved away; only our memories
are still gridded to the riverbanks. Even now
the edges do not fit together: the cities
in this city crack and shift beneath my feet.
Bridges flood, borders dangle, and I cannot
tie them up, situate myself.

Absent

I am looking for myself, frantically, the way you search for keys, checking your pockets twice, dumping your bag onto the countertops. I know I left myself here somewhere: sprawled beneath the dripping kitchen faucet, snaking through the labyrinth of pots and pans inside the cupboards, coalescing inside the solid orange mass of yesterday's macaroni.

I am buried alive in the rubble of minutiae. My transparent reflection in the window glass is tethered only by the lingering shred of habit. She turns her face away as my feet adhere permanently to the sticky linoleum.

I am paralyzed by the terrible smug certainty of salad forks stacked like bodies in the green plastic tray inside the drawer, my breath snagged and torn on the tines.

I was here when I last looked, but I haven't opened my eyes for years. This is the squalor that Sleeping Beauty woke to, the devastations and degradations of a hundred years. This is the way she tried to say *Where am I*, her lips cracked, her throat a dusty catacomb. We have both been betrayed by domesticity, by the flaws of our mothers. There will be no miracles, no rescue, no flaming sword to slice through the brambles and the briars, the hydrangea and the marigolds.

I am a story with an absent narrator, my skin turned inside-out. I am a somnambulant carcass, night-feeding on grief. I am an illusion, a sleight of mind. I've abandoned myself to this chaos of dishes and doorknobs, open-mouthed ovens and insidious filth, and I'm not really here at all.

AVAILABLE FROM CYCLOPS PRESS

For more information, visit www.cyclopspress.com. All titles are available in Canada thru Signature Editions, except where noted; international customers, please see our website.

Virgo Out Loud, Seán Virgo,
ISBN 1-894177-07-X, 16.95, Audio CD (Fiction)

Blindsight, Ricardo Sternberg,
ISBN 1-894177-03-7, 16.95, Audio CD (Poetry)

Necropsy of Love, Al Purdy,
ISBN 1-894177-01-0, 16.95, Audio CD (Poetry)

August Witch, Chandra Mayor,
ISBN 1-894177-12-6, 13.95, Book (Poetry)

Patrick Lane in Cab 43, Patrick Lane,
ISBN 1-894177-04-5, 16.95, Audio CD (Poetry)

In The First Early Days of My Death, Catherine Hunter,
ISBN 1-894177-14-2, 13.95, Book (Fiction)

Rush Hour, Catherine Hunter,
 ISBN 1-894177-08-8, 16.95, Audio CD (Poetry)

trains of winnipeg, Clive Holden,
ISBN 1-894177-10-X, 16.95, Audio CD (Poetry)
(thru Signature Editions or Endearing Records)

Fury: Fictions & Films, Clive Holden,
ISBN 1-894177-00-2, 11.95, Book (Fiction)
(from Arbeiter Ring Publishing in Canada)

transcona fragments, Jon Paul Fiorentino,
ISBN 1-894177-11-8, 14.95, Book (Poetry)

The Cyclops Review, Jon Paul Fiorentino, Ed.,
ISBN 1-894177-13-4, 13.95 Book (Anthology)

Local Scores, Terrance Cox,
ISBN 1-894177-09-6, 16.95 Audio CD (Poetry)